♦ ANIMAL, ♦

VEGETABLE,

✧ MINERAL

Also by Benjamin Harnett:

The Happy Valley: A Novel

Gigantic: Stories From the End of the World

◆ ANIMAL, ◆

VEGETABLE,

✧ MINERAL

POEMS BY
BENJAMIN HARNETT

Serpent Key Press

ANIMAL, VEGETABLE, MINERAL: POEMS

www.benjaminharnett.com

Published by Serpent Key Press, Cherry Valley, NY

www.serpentkey.com

ISBNs:
979-8-9867445-5-1 (Paperback)
979-8-9867445-0-6 (eBook)

LCCN: 2023920743

Cover and book design by Benjamin Harnett

10 9 8 7 6 5 4 3 2 1

ἐπάμεροι· τί δέ τις;
τί δ' οὔ τις; σκιᾶς ὄναρ

—

Living for a day; What is a man?
What is not a man?
The dream of a shadow.

—Pindar, 446 BCE

CONTENTS

♦ ANIMAL ♦

CONTENTS
(CONT'D)

❧ VEGETABLE ❧

CONTENTS
(CONT'D)

✧ MINERAL ✧

✧ ◆ ✧

PREFACE

THREE years ago I put together a slim poetry collection for my friends representing work from the past five or six years, had it privately printed, and ended up with a few extra copies. My wife Toni convinced me to stock them at her store, *Beacon Mercantile*, and they sold out.

Since the publication of my novel, *The Happy Valley*, people have been asking how they can read more of my work. With the help of *Serpent Key Press* I now have the opportunity to make this collection available again, and to a wider audience.

Because I couldn't help myself even if I wanted to, I've taken the opportunity to make changes here and there—some minor and some major. Do they represent improvements to the individual poems or the collection? —Maybe. But maybe not. They do, at least, make the work somewhat more representative of the state of my art and mind now, and this is all we can ask for a new edition, at least as long as its original author still lives and breathes.

I toiled on the original manuscript for this book from late 2019 through early 2020, just as the election season was heating up, and as the pandemic hit and changed and did not change everything, everywhere, all at once. In the original preface I hoped that readers of the future would encounter these poems in a world where things that could have gone badly instead went well. I am afraid it is still too early to tell.

—THE AUTHOR

CHERRY VALLEY, NY 2023

ORIGINAL PREFACE

T HE idea was simple: collect the three chapbooks of poetry I'd assembled for friends in 2016, 2017, and 2018 into one long book.

I would tweak a little, here and there, put poems into their right places, edit out an infelicity or two, and write this preface by way of apology and context. I must have known it wouldn't be so easy.

Even after I announced my plan, and got people to support it, putting myself "on-the-line," I hesitated. I entered a state of full-on, brutal procrastination; frozen from even opening the original files.

At last, when delay had grown into a beast of almost insurmountable embarrassment, I rolled up my sleeves. (Incidentally, this is 100% my usual writing process.) Originally one book, they had become manifestly three, and chafed at the recombination. Each one was a portrait of its time, and the state of my art, and this now, no less.

I have substantially rewritten a number of the poems, as you will see, and added new poems, and removed other ones. Some things read better, others worse, but what they have become is what they are now, a picture of my universe, here in early 2020, at the close of the Trump era and dawn of a somewhat better world, if things go well. If not…it has been nice.

L IKE the other ones, this is a self-published book. There was a time, for the ancients, when all books began in such a way. I am not purposefully bypassing the "gate-keepers" of poetry, whomever they are. No, I have worked diligently to publish individual poems, and sent out this and other manuscripts.

In the end this is but a monument to impatience and privilege: Impatience to see these poems in the frame of a book, privileged to be supported by my friends and to live in a time when such an object can be printed professionally. (A good-looking book is good for the ego.)

While I continue to send poems and manuscripts out, I offer this, in the meantime, as my "cut." It is not, God-willing, the last cut.

W HAT should you get from this book? From these poems? From poems in general? I don't know.

Animal, vegetable, mineral. These are the

taxonomic roots of our world. Do these poems propose, then, to cover the universe, the basis vectors of a three-dimensional space of being, yes. Or fill in, here, your preferred brand of bullshit, it will fertilize the same flowers to grow.

I hope only you find something to like in these pages. Maybe the sound the words make, one after the other, the echo they have, from line to line, beginning and end, poem to poem. The way the serifs nod and curl. Or you learn something, or wish to learn it. Or that flash of recognition: I have felt the same way once.

Some of these poems emerged fully formed, like strange gods growing out of the muck, others I keep whacking at with a hammer, adding bits, sawing away: images, stray thoughts, a word or two I put in the iPhone Notes App, or phrases I couldn't stop repeating to myself.

Like people, one or two might be quite good. None are all bad.

—THE AUTHOR

BEACON, NY 2020

C. PLINIUS CANINIO SUO S.

DELPHINUM gestatorem collusoremque puerorum in terram quoque extrahi solitum, harenisque siccatum, ubi incaluisset in mare revolvi.

Confluebant omnes ad spectaculum magistratus, quorum adventu et mora modica res publica novis sumptibus atterebatur. Postremo locus ipse quietem suam secretumque perdebat: placuit occulte interfici, ad quod coibatur.

—Plin. *Ep. ix.* 33

TO CANINIUS:

THE dolphin, who sported this way with the children and carried them on its back, would come to shore and dry itself in the sand and, as soon as it had warmed, return to the sea.

All the magistrates flocked to see the sight, and the extra cost of their stay could not be borne by the town. Moreover, the quiet and retirement of the place was ruined. It was, therefore, decided to kill, in secret, what had gathered the people there.

—Pliny the Younger, *Letters, ix.* 33

ANIMAL

EASTER SCENE

The neighbor kids
have painted an Easter scene
on their window: white rabbit,
green grass and trees,
red sun.

This last seems
to have bothered them.
They write an apology
in enormous block letters,
taking up a third of the pane:
"We don't have any yellow,"
with an arrow pointing,
to explain.

But the iron-oxidizing red,
the glassy smear of it
as it thins at the edges, this
is right for Easter. Apology
is right too, I think,

blood sweating
from the shoulder
as I carve the lamb.

THE LIGHT

The light after rain is a fire, saved
from the flood; blue oculus opening
in the clouds, like the hollow
of a reed. It lasts the space

of our walk before dark, becoming,
becomes the dark before: like waking
early enough you can but imagine
a dawn. Somehow

the hallway is just bright enough
to silhouette our cat staring us
on the dresser out of bed. The dim
glow hovering the stove,

a warm orange I have only lately
learned to name "orpiment"—the red
of the electric kettle when I flick
its switch to boil

are pale models for—what?—
while morning dresses itself
in fine, translucent layers.
Everything grows into

the light behind

the curtains as I draw them open,

until the nightlights wink

into day. There is

the old light, there is

the young: some lights go,

others stay. And there is

the light of our sun,

first red, then yellow,

burning off the fog on the hill.

After the flood, the wise man let

an otter dive—Nothing!

Then a beaver—Nothing, too.

Then a muskrat.

It dived deep, deeper,

down to the tip of a tree.

Back on the canoe it said,

"I could smell the land."

One more dive! I can almost

feel the light on my hand.

A FOX

A fox was struck

on the sloping road

above the rocky stream

where a logging trail led

to a field of horses—at the end

of it, people I knew

from high school kept chickens.

A few cars since must have done

what we had done, first:

slow, then arc around red body,

centered as it was in the lane.

But we stopped and walked back

to do what we could—

No mark on it, no injury

made plain. We stood, wondering

was death just the latest

trick the fox played?

A feeling doubled

as, when I took it by the nape

the fox almost leaned into my glove,

as if solicitous of touch,

and then I lifted, holding also

at the base of its brush.

Only then, in lifting,

did we see blood on the pavement

a fatal blot, color of its fur,

in the dappled shade. Then I laid it

gently upon the slanting shoulder,

whereupon it slid

through fallen leaves.

Then, I could have been convinced

that time is only mind's illusion,

and, if seeing again one fox,

or a swift-gliding pair,

picture scattered bones gathering

up the bank, growing muscle and hair,

warming into my hands, then to run

returned into the underbrush,

and chase, silently,

through fields

the long moon-shadows

while I grow quite young.

RODEO MONKEY

—TV Announcer: "Here comes the little monkey now!"

Rodeo Monkey's no joke. He's serious stuff.
He goes down, he'd be crushed.

Rodeo Monkey's not an intellectual type. He'd vote
Reagan, if he could.

Rodeo Monkey don't mind the crowd: he minds
the bull. Rodeo Monkey lives

with just one rule: hang tight, and never,
never let go. Sometimes,

yeah, he'll have a bad fall. Then he gets
a nice little smoke.

Sure he has a bit of a cough. But
who don't?

Rodeo Monkey loves grapes. Give him
one. Bite? Not after that fuss

with the kid. Yeah, he lives in a cage,
but does your cage have a TV set?

Question time's over, Lady.   Step aside.
Rodeo Monkey got the call

most monkeys don't get:
I'm Rodeo Monkey and Rodeo Monkey

was born to ride.

THE OCTOPUS

Out in the wary wideness
eight minds pull it.
Sunlight a fire: so reach
for the cool of dark
downwardness. Tentacles
go *self, self, self, self,* no!
Ah: big pebble. Lift to view:
This the one. Quick, back
to the closeness of home.

Felt air, once, a pitiless
flattening, bright roar
a kind of God. It worries
an old scar while balancing
the rock on a pile of them,
wrapped in self like a bone,
What was this self
but worry without comfort,
and ache for food?

To be a child again,
all eye and jelly, to drift
among the ignorant millions,
be swept up into a world-mouth

with one's family,

to dissolve, instead of being

one day torn by iron

and to die alone.

Still, upon reflection,

what this cave really needs

is another stone.

THE GREAT AMERICAN CIRCUS

"Is it sick?" I asked

after we had waited in line

for an interminable time

to see the pale-as-grass python

in a dingy aquarium, unmoving,

at the end of a trailer.

Dad didn't know what to say.

It was 1987, I was six. Next

it was on to the "big" tent,

where one elephant stood, shifting

its weight. Tiny Tim came out,

and did "Tip-Toe Through the Tulips"

in his trademark falsetto

to a scattering of bored kids.

After nine long years of this

he collapsed on a stage in Minnesota

and was, an hour later, dead

of a myocardial infarction,

an irreversible necrosis

of the heart. He was 64.

He'd had top hits—married
Miss Vickie on Carson—but
it had all faded, like his hair.
Born Herbert Khaury, I later learned
he could sing also in a deep baritone,
and recorded an album homage
to "the great crooners."

At the tail end of a second marriage
(to a Miss Jan), sallow, somewhat
bloated, he joined, as star
attraction, "The Great American Circus,"
a one-ring affair out of Tampa.

As he embarked,
he told the local paper,
"I made it once, I'd like
to make it one more time."

KING RAT

King Rat I am. My pelt is silver,
my iron paws end in black
nails, sickle-shaped as the moon.

To me, this concrete plain
is soft as spring rain.
My double shines up

from wet ground, all sparkle
at the verge. Gentle lashes frame
my still, open eyes.

I eat grit and hide a flaming tongue.
King Rat I am. I wear a crimson crown:
blood from a tiny dent in my skull.

Tomorrow my body is gone—
King Rat I am—me—and dead, but,
soaked into the sidewalk

this red shadow of my renown
will live me on, again
within thee.

BLOOD

Only when I turned, on accident,

(I never look)

and there it was,

my own blood

whirling up into the vial,

wet as the ocean, funneling

inward, did I understand

it for heirloom saltwater

as elementary school's film-strip

had explained:

that ancient cells surrounded

and carried it, sloshing onto land,

and how we could hear the ocean,

within us still, conch shell

to ear. This innocent

history of blood had flickered

from A/V cart–projector to portable screen,

a film setup better funding

would swap for a VHS player

to a small TV bolted-up in the corner.

So it is that everything

that becomes better

is also worse, and whatever we get,

we lose. That sea within us,

waiting to rush forth, finds only
a small glass void, and sky
but a drop-ceiling and fluorescence:
LabCorp, and the nurse saying,

"Shit! Sorry," as the needle
twists another bruise.

THYLACINE

The Tasmanian wolf, or tiger;

so called from its stripes we can now

regard only in black and white

like ribs along its haunches,

or prison garb. The last known

to the world, called "Benjamin,"

died on an abnormally cold night,

from exposure, 7 September 1936.

For a man to become a wolf

is a form of melancholy.

The wolf in its melancholy

becomes a man. Now,

they say, the search for those

thought extinct, is on,

as inconclusive sightings mount.

I want to believe! Some

remnants running—a distinctive

snout—the cryptid, found, says nature

can withstand our unnatural wasting,

mankind's beautiless, dead-

eyed wallow. Nothing

escapes, of course,

and nothing follows.

THE INVISIBLE BRIDGE

I am the invisible bridge the bear

tiptoes across (Oh, you thought, maybe,

he was jumping into the stream? Wrong!)

I am the invisible bridge the bear tiptoes

across however unlikely

that may seem. I am the tiny hand

that reveals itself to be a normal hand

when the man moves his arm. Convenient

how everything that is is only

a trick of perception. I am the sign that reads

"No clearance in niche." What do I know?

Maybe there's enough room

for the bear. They added over six-hundred words

to the dictionary this spring. I suppose

they shall have to remove some soon.

It is a bridge, invisible, the bear

tiptoes upon, it is a bridge that disintegrates

behind us, and grows under

our leather pads. And so the past is a green

bank out of all understanding,
and the future well, we can talk about it,

when we get there. We can talk about it
with the bear.

WILLIAM HARVEY'S DOGS

The old country doctor

can't shake his dream,

back in Med school, but hundreds of years past

together with William Harvey

vivisecting dogs—all night

the dogs' wild faces

their screams—blood gushing from dying hearts

in streams: Upon grueling extinction

of his first stray, Harvey's less-committed

predecessor Erasmus had written,

"Never again!"

Turn his face from the boy, the doctor things

let him enjoy the breakfast

of venison stew, steaming,

the still of the black morning outside,

the frost-licked panes. He wished

the boy would ask, "Why

do we have to kill?" Sometimes, almost always,

you must have the will to destroy

so that you can save the better part—

but to the boy he'd answer:

"We go hunting to forge a bond.

Together, in nature, to appreciate. I took

your father, and my father

took me." But the boy remains silent,
eating, then—
"Tell me again, Grandpa, what
makes the bullets go so fast?" So
he repeats the story:

trigger to sear
to spring-loaded hammer,
pin to primer, gunpowder, bursting flame,
the boy makes a finger gun, goes "Blam!"
The doctor's wife watches.
As through lavender light they depart,
shotguns broken over shoulders,
camo draped in orange. Later years,
she remembers of their going,
the chestnut tree in the drive,
an armlike branch begins to tremble
as it sways above the van,

and, of its woody hand,
such an index finger curls,
as if to pull
fire upon the world.

BEE–FATHER*

- I. -

January: "I felt the hive, it was warm."
March: "I rapped the hive, it buzzed."
But by May the hive is silent. The bees
have died.

So Dad's off to Morris, an hour-plus southwest,
to give it another go:
he makes his hand follow a wave
to show hill after hill—"And No NPR for miles."
Just the droning of his truck.

I was always afraid of them, bees;
nearby buzzing would freeze my heart.
Now I delight to watch them
harvest flowers, determinedly. What
transformation, Dad's emergence, in white bee-suit
patched with duct tape, from the basement,
face shrouded by netting, tin smoker
in one hand. How I would watch

crouched behind his powder-blue Datsun
as he space walked through bees

*So the Carpathians call the "master of the hives."

drowsed by smoke, ships or inverted stars
black against white to take their combs.
Then the extractor—enormous, much-used, tin;
it had a faulty bearing or something, so
that it shuddered hard
as you turned the crank to spin.

Such spinning, even uneven, would drive honey out,
dark sweetness flecked with pale wax shards
and the hint of pollen.
You'd fill mason jars from the iron spout.

Are bees messengers, buzzing out transmissions
from here to the world
of souls?

Or is the soul a bee, always working,
always humming on
incessantly?

- II. -

O, honey! Sole sustenance of poets!
To be poured by the little muses upon the lips,
skimming the mind with amber,
so that yesterday

and forty years whence are embalmed together

like Alexander, in honey and wax,

with cassia, and cinnamon:

now and when Wayne Graham

and my father brought the self-same extractor

up East Hill to "The Committee,"

(Allen Ginsberg's poetry farm)

so that Peter Orlovsky and his brother Julius,

a ten-year catatonic, could harvest

unspoiling sweetness from their bees,

and helped the pair slide frames

of honeycomb in as sunset bore up

a milk-pale sky with pink

and orange and crimson red.

Shirtless Julius began to dance a circle

as they cranked the extractor in turns,

so it whirled and banged

with its clanking metal speech

shuddering out golden honey and Julius,

from mind-clamped silence

whooped, at first uneasily, then loudly yelled

all joyous in the swollen dark,

a wild animal, growling shadow

against the flickering of a campfire

and burning joint or cigarette-ends

pointed neon on silhouetted faces.

It was the very next day

I am told

that Julius chose,

or was inspired,

after so long silent

to speak.

MOTH/MONEY

Like in a vintage cartoon,

some crumpled bills fall upward

from my open wallet and swarm

the lamp, beating such hard

shadow into my chest

that it flutters. Another day,

I'll crush them into my palm,

pull green-gleaming wings taut

and smooth them into a bed

of small possibility, except

for that one the cat got,

carried gingerly, evoking

the desperate, papery flap

of a moth, caught, momentarily,

and lost behind the radiator.

And me? Down on my knees,

with broom handle sweeping

the narrow dark in need.

PEOPLE WATCHING

The news is an empty plate

I push away, residue

of brunch's steak and eggs

a bloody shadow

lightened by a yolk glaze.

Some squirrels seem bored,

on the oak across the way,

heads cocked, people watching,

the cascade of hipsters

dragging kale across their plates,

to them indistinguishable

as cattle. Like the rest

I put plate aside, pretend

to work: headphones, laptop,

caffè latte and all. Remember

when rumor comprised

many specific, evil incidents,

each with a single, hateful villain,

instead of all this mass,

this faceless calamity,

these oceans of dread.

So there was that putty-faced dentist

who flew to Africa to bag a lion.

It ranked especially bad

because the trackers had lured

out of a nature preserve,

for the good doctor's bow—

it had a homing-collar, and a name.

The lion, Cecil, slinks through tall grass

follows bloodscent idly, drowsy

in all that sun. His taste

knows no boundaries, his hide

no cuts, until the quick jab

of that ridiculous arrow,

let loose with the nonchalance

of the pricking of a gum.

Now the real work began

as the guides followed his fleeing

wounded path, night and day, and at last

finish him with a knife,

for their good suburban-

USA hunting-man,

and hack Cecil's dead

trophy-head from its neck.

"In my early animal behavior work,"

says Temple Grandin,

"I noticed that cattle often balked

and refused to walk over shadows

or pass a coat hung on a fence.

A horse that had alcohol tossed in its eye

during a visit from the vet became

afraid of black hats, while white hats

were safe. He had been looking

at a black hat when

the alcohol was thrown."

(I do not have a sense if this is normal

in a horse's life or accidental:

such fragmentary knowing

characteristic of our age.)

Grandin, in her hope

for less cruelty designed a new

kind of slaughterhouse—You are standing

in the field with your kind,

grass at your ankles, tag in

your ear. (As the cows go down the chute

they often come in the same order

as they were tagged the year before.)

Your shoulders find you fenced,

tin walls hold you. At every turn

your sense of being here or there is lost,

you become a tunnel-loving worm.

The wall gives away, so unseen to your following

is the bolt or shock or knife takes you

from the day. It is how you would almost

wish to go.

Now the way is like a jaw,

and the taking, a socket of pain, uncalled-for,

as though this dentist,

shabby pretender to God, yanked a tooth

that had no flaw,

while some people watching in smocks,

hook your carcass,

then the saw.

HEY, YOU NEVER KNOW

The electric spark

on the sidewalk

is half a cellophane wrapper

from a pack of cigarettes,

skittering through discarded

scratch-offs, face-down,

yellow backs so many leaves

like that carpet

of glue-traps our super

left in the basement

when we rented that space

in Manhattan. We'd see

oversized roaches perfectly transfixed

except for one anxious feeler

probing hypnotically a sea

of impossibility. Once

I came upon a mouse—

writhing—it had pushed itself

forward, in desperate

centimeters trail

of black excrement

prison-tears in its wake.

I flicked off the light,

walked backward up the stairs,

complicit with those

who would condone such an end

to a life of fruitless struggle—

On what grounds?

That having ourselves

won the lottery of being

we lack deeper understanding?

That we do not love ourselves

enough to love

another animal?

THIS IS FINE, DOG

Took the express today, and by God

it was—express and then some.

Was that elation, as we blew through normal stops,

Cold Spring, Garrison, Peekskill,

Cortlandt, even Croton-Harmon,

or existential dread?

Even so, we raced while fogged in,

befogged too, all,

only a pattern of ripples

separating river from sky,

an occasional island

floating past like a narrowed eye

of stone and roots

and fall leaves.

Some people's heads lolled

in sleeping, and the same exhaustion

played over me. When interior doors

opened I felt I could see

the whole length of the train

sloping downward from me

a pale yellow caterpillar, swollen

with humans,

dreaming in a gray cocoon.

I took out my notebook, so many

lined pages, every intention

of putting it to work,

but only stared

at a sticker it has,

a panel from that famous cartoon.

"This is fine," the dog says

with a grin, with a jaunty hat.

He contemplates a cup full

of the blackest java,

while his roof fills with smoke,

and bright orange flames saw

into the frame.

This is fine, dog. One for the ages.

C. PLINIUS TACITO SUO S.

U SUS ille sole, mox frigida, gustaverat iacens studebatque; poscit soleas, ascendit locum ex quo maxime miraculum illud conspici poterat. Nubes—incertum procul intuentibus ex quo monte (Vesuvium fuisse postea cognitum est)—oriebatur, cuius similitudinem et formam non alia magis arbor quam pinus expresserit.

Nam longissimo velut trunco elata in altum quibusdam ramis diffundebatur, credo quia recenti spiritu evecta, dein senescente eo destituta aut etiam pondere suo victa in latitudinem vanescebat, candida interdum, interdum sordida et maculosa prout terram cineremve sustulerat.

—Plin. *Ep. vi.* 16

TO TACITUS:

M Y uncle took in the sun, then had a cold bath; he had eaten while reclining and was beginning to study. He asked for his slippers and went up to a place from which the marvel was most conspicuous. A cloud—it was uncertain to those watching from afar from which mountain (afterwards it was known to have been Vesuvius)—was rising, which resembled nothing so much as a pine tree.

For, being raised up high on a very tall trunk, it was spreading out like branches. Because, I believe, having been carried forth by a fresh blast and then forsaken by a diminishing force, or even conquered by its own weight, it was dissipating to the sides, sometimes white, sometimes dimly dark and speckled, according to the earth or ash it had borne.

—Pliny the Younger, *Letters, vi.* 16

VEGETABLE

TREE REPAIR

Arborists—anodyne, officious moniker
for who were once called tree-doctors or -surgeons—
"experts" in all perennial, woody plants, which amounts
to knowing what to clip, what to saw, and when
to suggest a new planting

to replace an ailing giant, out of which,
implored to save, the best will hollow
the rot of age, trowel in concrete,
add some PVC pipe to drain:
engineer, architect, carpenter,
what any doctor is, really,

just shoring up the trunk, and keeping
strong the flow. Trees build
themselves out of air, take carbon
from CO_2 and knit it
into wooden flesh, veins, and bones.

We, too, build ourselves, in time
require shoring up, are good
as long as we can stand.
Then, some green-shirt,
with a canvas painters-bag full

of awls and plastic tubes will squint
and say, "He'll go another hundred
years if he will go a day."

Lightning fodder, useless as fuel,
all twisted and losing bark, and how
the Christian missionaries,
those early-day saints, delighted
in bringing down Donar's Oak and Irminsul,
while their flocks wept in secret.
In Douglaston, L.I., people felt bad, too,
as that ancient, maybe oldest,
tree came down over a period
of several days, supervised.

Arborists couldn't say how old it was;
You can't tell, really, once the center
has gone.

Now there are condos where it stood,
and a nice sloping lawn.

SUN WORSHIP

Dawn. Life here is not
how you have heard, although
I just walked through the waft
of garbage from an exploded bag
of formless filth a truck let fall
and someone hit.

Hump-winged with craning,
blackened neck, a chimney sits
atop a brownstone house
like the lost eagle standard
of a Roman legion slaughtered
in shaded, Teutonic woods.

Other protrusions are watchful,
vent-pipes long-closed, satellite dishes,
piles of brick, their dull flashing
stringy with black-tar vines like blood.
Today I'd welcome even
a discouraging word.

The sound of a child unwrapping candy,
is three clever birds, peeling foil
from a fallen taco. They pause
as I near, but do not leave,

pink blossoms of pork revealed

between cilantro leaves' shading green.

A church, in gas-station letters, says

SUN WORSHIP 11AM. There is no

more fitting god, saluted daily from birth

to Icarusian fall, when live swifts sweep

insects from the rays, and man's crude,

inanimate flocks at last go dark.

THE DEATH OF BALDER

*Balder, Odin's blameless, shining son, of whom all good things could
be said, was killed through the treachery of Loki by a harmless dart
of mistletoe: a tragedy for the Æsir, and harbinger of Ragnarök,
twilight of the Gods.*

With my beer, with the dog,
waiting for the grill to heat,
in that *Family Dollar* chair,
bothered by some mosquitoes
hovering, like tiny spears,
or like a bomb I saw
in the news-photo, frozen
over Palestine, ready to feed.

Oak, ash, maple, linden, ivy,
a patch of grass the size
of a prison-cell our landlady's brother
mows, strangling kudzu, high up
a sphere of mistletoe, waxy, dark;
one neighbor's plot an overgrown ruin,
the other bare concrete, the green
deepening, the sky a curtain.

Is life just the sum of all our debts
and what to one is owed?
The wind gusts. The leaves show
all at once their pale palms,
a mass supplication, then shiver
back, and stir, and say, "How
have we, all of us, gotten so old?"

A firefly snaps orange then
snuffs out. Scraps of newsprint still
intact in the ash the rising
flames kicked into the charcoal-pan,
one with a child's face, singed,
drags along the flagstone,
turns down. Soon

it will be winter,
and the mistletoe will shine
from the mass of naked limbs
a spray of yellow leaves,
a golden bough.

ALMOST 9PM

Since you left, the radiators

sigh and sigh. The crooked

lamp's amber shade makes

bright cheeks of light

upon our wall. The plant

that hangs beside (a pothos)

is all tangled-up like hair. I first saw

the other day on the very tip

of the last leaf of every

tumbling strand, perfect, crystal bulbs

of water stand. Do you suppose

this water ever falls, or does

the air just rub it dry?

SHIPWRECKS

I have been awake, dreaming of shipwrecks
ancient planks unraveling from broken ligatures,
"Marseille, Marseille, Marseille, Agay-
Anthéor—(avaient perdu leur . . . had lost
their . . ." Underwater, the sound of waves above
seethes and rushes, no—
underground on a subway ride,
and everyone, and I, are tired, and tired
nod together like kelp, that rushing,
air from an eyebrow-window
cocked. I feel pressure against my leg.
"À partir de 600 av. J.-C," light speckles
moldering wood, rolling like a voice,

"What is it you're reading?
Fiction, or non-? I just want to talk to you."
A thick, friendly face, reeking of beer,
one eyetooth a gap, gaping. I cower
into the satiny sheening pages, down,
six-hundred years before Jesus Christ.
"I know about books," he says,
"I just want to know, is it Stephen . . . ?"
Trailing off, he gives up, hands resting,
leather crabs on the bright denim
of his knees. Below the cuffs,

his new sneakers have black and yellow laces,

twining eels with neon backs, I wish,

to say something in return to him,

something like "Yes," as in, I too

am a beautiful wreck, shattered in sand,

drifting with the tides.

LAST CUT

Through a quiet sprawl,

the balanced light,

the day,

this early fall,

dull, rust-spotted mower

chugging along,

I cover the lawn,

a last cut before

winter.

Up to the yard's limit

edging, when the blade

clips a fallen apple,

just so:

speckled red

springing

to snow.

SECURITY QUESTIONS

Who is your favorite celebrity?
What is the make and model of your dream car?

What is your favorite land-dwelling animal?
Where are we going? Is it far?

What was the last name
of your academic advisor in college?

Where does the relative who lives
farthest away from you reside?

And you, are you living, or have you died?
What type of dog/cat food do you typically

buy? What was the make and model
of your first cell phone? Is it true

everybody living, lives alone?
Who is your favorite artist? What was

the first musical instrument you learned to play?
Can we ever be forgiven

for making that one, big mistake? What

was the last name of your kindergarten

teacher? What can we do in life,
if we don't understand the stakes?

What was it that the serpent said
in the garden to Eve?

Why must we leave?

CATASTROPHE

We talk about wreckage, a hillside of trees stacked
the saws have been buzzing and snarling for weeks.
Trees come down like great knuckle cracks.
Another development with "river views."
A catastrophe. There have been others:
the election, something wrong with the fridge,
your Grannie passing.

We are heading into a catastrophe of clouds;
some storm kicked up over Lake Ontario
or Erie. A dead tree is weathered into bone;
some cars flicker, a procession of candles
parallel the train; red-and-green running lights,
a single tractor trailer against the green base
of the mountain. So that's night,

I dream we are together, though we will meet
somewhere below the Middle West. Past midnight
in Ohio, the carriage fills with Amish,
moonlight hollows their faces, but they smile,
read magazines. We pronounce it
with such overweening, personal pride:
"catastrophe."

It is only the turning point, the last unwinding.
Of the barren hillside, I regret only the no more
deer at dusk, frozen in my passing.
Mule-eared and white muzzle shining, I could run
my hand along its bristle-furred back.
Life goes on. The longer we have,
the more we lack.

HOME

It might not be surprising to you
as it was for me to learn
that a bird makes no home.
I often think of them, out in the rain.
This is my home. There is dust

in the corners. A hole in the sheetrock
I have to fill, then sand, then paint.
We bought some furniture
for the porch, but it's too cold out
now to use. A dog likes to sleep
surrounded on three sides.

Then I recall: for a bird,
the sky is solid—a bird's house
is larger than mine. We built
a fire in the yard, and drank beers
the night our cat died. My coat
still reeks of smoking pine. Fire is

the soul of the wood, raveling
back into the air, the trunk,
the living built to house itself
over time. A tree is its own house,
and a bird's, and mine.

MILKWEED

Some things you feel
to have always known:
snap a green stalk, it bleeds white.
Crush a leathery pod
in your palm, silk threads crawl
living through the tight slits
of your hand.

But have you really seen its flowers,
set like blushing cabochons
in a cocktail ring,
or the yellow, white, and black
caterpillars, flexing as they feed.
Life is unexpected, strange,
how the insects make
an emerald fixture
of themselves, only

to crack out. Crushed, wavering
flesh falters then open
like a cape: the winking monarchs fly,
I remember there were more
by many, in the air,
when Maude took me
foraging. Was she seven,

and I five? The young leaves
and pods we plucked

put in a cast-iron pan
of water on the cast-iron stove
I could barely reach,
were tender and sweet.
(So I now recall,
could it be true?)
As we ate, larval in our form,
I felt an itching in my shoulders
as if preparing themselves

for some great unwrapping,
some reveal—childhood's
secret wings.

A SHORT HISTORY OF FINANCIAL EUPHORIA

Sometimes at our grocery store,

bundled, bright and fragrant,

splashed in zinc buckets, wrapped

in cellophane, will be

some tulips, and, if feeling rich,

say finding a forgotten coat-pocket $10,

I'll secure a bunch.

The beauty of certain tulips is a virus

in the bulb; petals push away languid

green to rise heavy with

their own perfume, white as a flag

and shot-through with that signal

of their infecting strain, lovely

crimson veins.

Sober economists maintain

that tulipomania was not

nearly so outrageous

as stories claim. But I always

think to how, one blue night,

a Dutch sailor

mistaking tulip bulb for onion

slice by slice

consumed

the riches

of a life.

SAY IT TO THE MOUNTAIN

Here upon this dry shore,

narrow spit of land,

the fish is so out of place

I almost miss seeing it,

in the shadow,

as it strains its whole body,

stops, and strains again.

The fisherman who caught it

is hidden by the ruddy trunk

of a tree. He has tossed

some smaller ones to his left,

they are already dead,

iridescent sheaths befouled

in their throes by sand.

What, now so squeamish?—

the rest of the animals

ask. But these poor fish—

you can't even eat them.

(Thanks, *General Electric,*

we salute you!)

The fisherman glares at me

as he ties on another

lure. An older woman
is picking up scattered garbage
into a bag. Two yuppies have biked
out here with their kid; are smoothing
out a blanket to picnic.

It is the first real "beautiful day"
of spring. It is all so natural,
really, this
defiant indifference.
The big fish still striving,
hopeful of water.
The man drawing a circle
around himself,
in the sand. Aren't we
the fish, each
learning, slowly,
how not to breathe?

For wasn't it Jesus himself
who withered
with his command
an innocent tree,
the blameless fig?

THE BRIDE EXTRUDES

The bride extrudes

as from the stones of the wall

like buttercream frosting

dabbed from confectioner's steel-toothed

nozzle into a flower,

or like a real flower waking

in layers

from the heavy weight

of its enfolding bud. We are caught

between her growing beauty

and the impassable end

on that long balcony that, unroofed,

caps a side of Siena's unfinished

cathedral. It is so long ago

the camera of the photographer

who precedes her, walking backward,

is large as its own church

in his hands—lofty, architectural.

Vera and I waver

at our distance, bride's dress

beating like a flag in the wind

the groom a shadow

to her brilliance

similar to the deeply imperfect

suitors Vera had listed that her age allows

(and I am, briefly one).

I do not believe

in poetry, then,

but believe right there

before we slip past the wedding party

like a lost thought that

I could believe

again,

then descend.

THE TREES ON THE ISLAND
(IN THE RIVER)

The trees on the island

in the river bristle

in the sinking sun

like fur on the rump

of an animal.

Is it a bear, the size

of your longing? And what

of the fish it's after?

This love, this living,

as big as the land.

In the mind of their roots

the trees on the island

in the river think

of me as some fur,

if they think of me

at all, that is,

the fur of leaves,

all pore and opening.

Pity we are not

only trunks,

not rooted to this island

in the river, not free

like the trees to settle

but tossed in the wind,

bound to be

thrust against whatever

we come upon, and washed

in shadow or dried

to a husk

by tomorrow's sun.

*MEDITATIONS**

Among the Quadi, at the river Gran,

in my war-tent, light going dim,

scratching Greek letters

to parchment

like troops in serried array

I march against

the sad disorder of my mind.

Whatever I am, it is

a little flesh, and breath.

Whosoever claimed he would

live forever—I finally feel the cold.

Are soothsayers right? I doubt

that soul-fire traces out for us to read

its shining secrets

in the whither-which-way flights

of birds. Yet, I allowed the men

to throw a pair of lions

into the Rhine. In their swimming

we should all be saved.

Philosophy is the last refuge

of rich youths allergic to work.

*Marcus Aurelius was Emperor of Rome from 161 CE until his death in 180 CE. While campaigning in Germany he wrote a book of Stoic philosophy, called *Meditations.* He was succeeded by his son, Commodus, cruel and indifferent, whose murder is fixed at the beginning of Rome's long decline.

But have I labored, Fronto,* hard.

Men die. Wives betray. Your only

living child looks upon you

with the glassy eyes of a beast.

Your lazy, adoptive father

railing against the Parthians

on his death-bed, for a hundred

diplomatic slights I scarcely care,

sends the golden statue of misfortune

into your chamber

and says, as he passes, "Lead!"

I scorn those for whom

life is lived

only for the world after

but I have done my duty and then some.

Let coins be placed upon my eyes,

and at the cypress tree† by the liver Lethe

offering forgetfulness

I will drink.

*His tutor, with whom he kept up a long correspondence.

†Souls were compelled to drink a deep draught, fatal to memory, and requisite
for reincarnation.

HOLLOW

"In the hollow of my hand" may be

a locus of sheer fact, dictionary

definition and all that; but I grew up

in a hollow, in a house in new woods

at the foot of one hill and head

of another. Now, a pair of beavers

damming the stream

have swollen it into the valley,

it laps the bases of the grand, old willows,

will kill them, eventually, by slow rot.

It was goat-farm once, all of it

shorn clean of tree and branch.

Just brilliant meadow, a one-room

schoolhouse for the children,

blacksmith shop,

the white farmhouse

with green shutters,

a horse-and-trap to town.

My parents built a home there,

with their own hard labor,

I can almost see it at the corner

where the crease of my lifeline

makes a road through my hand.

Metaphora means "moving."
Modern Greeks splash it
across their trucks.
The hollow is a metaphor,
and, like the movers,

I'll fill it with all this stuff.

C. PLINIUS SURÆ SUO S.

ET mihi discendi et tibi docendi facultatem otium praebet. Igitur perquam velim scire, esse phantasmata et habere propriam figuram numenque aliquod putes an inania et vana ex metu nostro imaginem accipere. Ego ut esse credam…

Erat Athenis spatiosa et capax domus…Per silentium noctis sonus ferri, et si attenderes acrius, strepitus vinculorum longius primo, deinde e proximo reddebatur: mox apparebat idolon, senex macie et squalore confectus, promissa barba horrenti capillo; cruribus compedes, manibus catenas gerebat quatiebatque.

—Plin. Ep. vii. 27

TO SURA:

THIS leisure allows time for you to give, and me to receive, some learning. I very much would like to know whether ghosts exist, with their own particular forms and powers, or do you think they are empty phantasms of our own fearful imagination? I am inclined to believe…

There was, at Athens, a large house…Often the silence of night would clang with iron, and to the attentive it became the rattling of chains; first at a distance, then approaching. At last there appeared the phantom of an old man, thin, dirty, with a long shivering beard, shaking the shackles on his arms.

—Pliny the Younger, Letters, vii. 27

MINERAL ✦

✦ ✦ ✦ ✦ ✦ ✦ ✦

GRAND OPENING

It has been their "Grand Opening" so long
the hanging pennants have faded
from bright primaries to pastel:
the overall effect as the ribbons
lie against the green rust–colored
building is of a rare bird amidst
the foliage of a remote forest,
though we are only so far
as farthest Queens. They are brothers

or if they weren't when it began
they are brothers now in the minds
of anyone left to remember—who is whom,
exactly? Were they immigrants?
I guess they were. The boy
who threw the brick thought so.
I thought windows were supposed
to shatter now, like sugar-glass
for safety, but it is a jagged hole,

a wicked break as if an emptiness
in space could just explode.
We are all immigrants, I don't mean
just here, in America, I mean

our consciousness comes

from some other shore—Reality

ticks along beside us,

alien, unsure.

It will never accept us. Some make

less of it, and others more.

MYCENÆ

Ten years ago (twenty now?)
this land tilts,
burning toward the sea:
it is mounds in the groves
of spring cuttings; afire
they flame and flicker
through branches of half-silvered
leaves while the sky
is a net of black smoke
tossed over me.

Students massed at the gate
craning necks up to headless
lions in the lintel,
I thread them with a *signomi*
and step, alone, up age-smoothed
wagon-track, crumbled walls jutting
beside the path, like a jawbone
half-hidden in the grass.

And I feel, with my tongue,
the deep pits of my own molars
as I pass. At the height
of the citadel where a stone doorway,

blocked by an iron gate,

houses a stairway descending

darkly into hill, it breathes

a cool air that

brushes the skin at my neck,

a whisper from deep time,

that dull-tin sea

of tragedy

Agamemnon's queen

said was wet

and would never dry.

SIX OF ONE...

I am descending into *Whole Foods*,

with a gift card that needs must be spent,

also inward hope of picking up

some bourgeois contentment.

It is the Thursday

after a black customer

was beat up at one of their stores

(I should say choked,

slammed against the floor,

brutalized by security because

of a disagreement over an EBT card

the sales associate would not,

presumably incorrectly, accept—)

It is Easter time (I think:

I am writing months later,

and if it was not near

sacrifice and resurrection, I feel content

to move the date to such a symbolic

moment, much as the early Christians did.)

At escalator's conclusion, people

of a fancy aspect all clustered

around the carts seem to writhe

like mating snakes. I am absorbed

by the knot, then ejected.
I find myself propelled forward
until I am at last left alone, standing
in a long aisle one side of which is
a display of naked, white eggs that
won't end. Empty cartons explain

to the novice their need to be filled—
the eggs, high-domed and cold as ice,
in longing, I felt, they glowed.
"Oh, Duck-eggs," the checkout clerk says,
correcting his own ignorance,
and mine. I had selected six,
clutching at them in desire—oblong gems
each having a single tag stuck on it
impressed with red numerals
the purpose of which I found myself
unable to guess—(lot-numbers, perhaps,
at the auction of an antique statue garden,
carved marble eggs, next lot:
stone Nereides; then effigies of Pan).

Such an egg Ophion enwrapped
at Orphic dawn, that birthed the entire
universe, an expanding horror
still going on.

BIOGRAPHY

They were unctuously good children:

eager to please, clever at school

(as was I), or unprepossessing

and exceptionally dull (this is

the insect-like trajectory). She was

a rare beauty who hid her wit

until it cut someone down like a blade.

He toiled on in obscurity. She had

her work stolen. They were admired,

but only by those in the know.

Until now. Every moment of their lives

followed ordinarily every moment

that came before. Some were born rich

and we marvel when they make much

of having much to begin with.

A few rose from the absolute bottom.

Every biography ends the same way—

death of the main character. Though

there is some variety in the cause.

There were always moments of insight.

Voyages or pivotal meetings. But a lot
of dull living, churning meat and vegetables
into shit, chain smoking, four cups of coffee.
Sciatica pain when they sit. So unsatisfying
every biography is, as if by design,

a secret conspiracy to hide
whatever formulas exist—I mean by what
application, what chemical concatenation,
how one might actually take
the base metal of our bodies

and transform it
to gold.

I HAVE

I have never been so tired in my whole life.
The mountains run across

the river—pointing

like a knife. Forlorn

boathouses perched out on rotting piers.
Empty lots of naked scrub.

A water tower.
A column of fire.
The lattice of clouds makes

a sparkling fishmouth,

the intervening atmosphere,

twinkling distant lights.
Crepuscular, this stand of trees.
In my hands, a paperback—
yellowing leaves.

Everything I have
and everything
I need.

GROUNDS

"Grind your beans to the consistency
of bread-crumbs,"
online instructions for preparing
the "best" coffee
in a French press exhort.

And yesterday's errant
grounds *do* stand out
on the countertop in blue dawn
like Hansel's path back
to . . . something?

I should say more, not just
that rising up from fizzy bloom,
as water poured up to the half,
30-seconds off-boil,
is a scent that carries me back

to those early mornings before school,
cocooned in sheets, when Dad's coffee
would sputter and hiss
into the glass urn, that it recalls
the taste of my first coffees,

sipped from styrofoam, rotten with sugar,

having secured a ride

with my cousin to the self-consciously

beatnik school-sponsored open-mic

lost, even then, to time.

Nor even that, cup by cup,

our morning coffees shine

through moonlight—that we follow

their path, childish yet,

though we killed the witch.

Heading back toward, but

uncertain of the home

which once

cast us

out.

READING *LEAR*

CORDELIA Time shall unfold what plighted cunning hides, Who covers faults, at last with shame derides. Well may you prosper.

ON seat-back, on "moving-map," the dark paw of Michigan rendered doubly unreal when city names are cast into Chinese. A neon ribbon trails our plane as though affixed to an arrow shot by a colossus over the smooth shoulder of our earth, continuously unspooling with a silent whoosh. I awake in a halo, reading lamp still active, half-disbelieving this isn't all a dream, Pelican *Lear* open in my hands, on the blanket, on my knees: *I have always been flying.* The black lip beneath the window-shades is a void, and the flickering topograph: a printout of my imagination; my book the only book that has ever been.

A little shake of turbulence which rattles the fuselage snaps me into reality, or is it that the names of the cities snap back to English on the screen? Grand Rapids, Ann Arbor, Saginaw, Detroit. Cordelia, in real life, un-obsequious daughter whose inheritance was blotted from the map like she had never been, conquered all with her army and put her father back as king. Shakespeare wrote it more right than real: when you have lost your way on the map, the lines that are drawn, names that are pricked a bloody shaking shows are wounds no sudden recognition can heal.

TWO YEARS BEFORE THE MAST

I am trying to tell you about the time

we lived behind the store

on an inflatable mattress (after a while

it sprung a leak so that, even pumped

firm as anything you

would wake as if rolling on

the sea, and gradually sink

to the floor). It was

two years before the Mast

brothers were un-bearded as faux-hipster

chocolate-frauds. We had a booth, once

or twice, near them, at *Brooklyn Flea.*

At the time, I had a thick red

beard myself, there never seemed time

to shave. I had gotten so thin

from stress under my clothes Toni joked

about "pioneer days."

Monday was our Sunday. We

swabbed the decks with Murphy's

and Windex, and a microfiber duster.

Unfurled the scarves.

Someone knocked one Monday morning

on the gate, it was
Anjelica Huston. I helped
her pick out two leather bags while
the coffee maker
sputtered fresh *Café Bustelo.*
At night the whole place
would glow from the streetlamps.

We stacked the back with hides.
Our friend Laurel dated
the "Pickle King" from Detroit,
who acted in some commercials
too. We'd meet them out
then come back late

to the store, where we clung
to each other, like to a spar
cast away in the frothy main,
until we drifted, finally
home.

THE WHITE SUPREMACIST
(AND I)

The white supremacist and I bond

on our love of small dogs

and that flock of sparrows

in our neighborhood

we both feed. For some reason he is telling me

about oatmeal—the kind they stopped carrying

at *Key Food.* He scatters it

for them on a glass patio table. I imagine the birds

a blanket on the hedge, soft grey, striped,

hopping from safety to sustenance

in fours and fives.

The first difference between us

is I do not try to chase away

the squirrels; "I'll kill those fuckers," he says.

Oh, and the *SS* tattoo,

and the one that says "9/11 ftw,"

and the casual violence with which

he calls me from across the street,

pulls me like a magnet to the fence.

His black vest has a patch

of the Confederate flag:

"The South Will Rise Again."

My dog begins to pant

and pace, and to whine

beside me. I am frozen

in hate though I feel

he is nothing but a sad old man.

His "old lady" has his precious dog—

therapy for her, she's

going into the hospital,

"to get the crazy shocked out."

"I'm going to give her one last

chance, then take Missy back,

and she can fuck off."

I have crushed the weeds

I was plucking to paste

in my right hand.

I want to stove his face in.

Our hold on a just life

is that thin.

YAHOO! ANSWERS

How is babby formed? Is true love real?

What makes the woman underground?

Can jet fuel burn steel? I eat massive amounts

of spaghetti. Why

do my ancestors complain?

The bone twists in the fire as it burns. A shadow

on the liver says the King will die. Enlil

wrestles with a bull.

Why can't birds fly into space? Does the God

in the Mountain House control our fate?

I've heard of a place called Rům,

far to the west of here,

where all the people live as ghosts.

Why shouldn't animals carry guns?

Where do our lives go when our body is done?

Can a dream reveal what is, or what

will be, or could it be just disordered excitation

of the imagination, brought on

by stress?

Will a human ever walk on the sun?

ROGER AILES IS DEAD

So the angel Drudge proclaims.
Let him fondle on in hell, I say.
Today, the river is a prosaic poem,
rippling, iridescent.

Cranes nod against a long, half-built
shed on the railroad steading, empty
windows gape, girders crossing
impending shadow.

Iron rails red as old blood are stacked
like ladders up the gravel bed.
We crawl forward, the train. How dull
it all is. Every day the same

big bottle nestled in low shrubs
on the bank by the stairs. Part-full
of *Colt 45* or urine. Nothing will tell.
Baseball is a wreck—

my parents' gardens were terraced
with old railroad ties. Oak or pine
bathed in creosote. We took flat stones
from the wrecked barn foundation,

replaced wood with dry-stacked walls.
The black earth opens, draped in
worms. The bottle, glass neck broken,
never had a head.

SEVEN SLEEPERS

- I. -

Either a shepherd roused them,

or they had just tired of sleep

after seven generations of it.

A little dog was with them, a guard

for the centuries, or was it only

a dog-shaped stone?

Woke, they shuffled from their cave,

seven sages, into the village.

The people marveled at their long beards,

and the ancient coins of Decius

with radiate-crown they slipped

from aged fingers for foodstuff and wine.

And when the priest told them

that Christ had won His final victory

over Rome, directly

they died.

- II. -

I stumbled up from the dark—
visitor to what had been my home—
into a bright emptiness, silent except for what
the guidebook calls "a drowsy, rambling warble"
frequently "in a grove of shade trees
on the bank of a stream,"
the call of a thrush.

From open windows, September,
summer's last flourishing,
the sound rolled like water
over pebbles in a dream.
In the Northeast it was a decades-rare
glorious day.

I listened to that birdsong
tripping through stillness
while I made tea, then clicked
the radio on. Only dead air
met me. Then a voice that cracked—
it said, "I think the second tower
is gone."

ZENOBIA

It is a ruin on a ruin on a ruin, it is my life.
Palymra. They say the spring, that sacred slit
in the desert that makes a lip of hard water
from chalky rock, has vomited up
all the gold you ever offered it.

A woman, like a city, is ruined from birth.
These pleasure-gardens and arcades, the endless stone
temples have gone on too long, already.
I strap on a leather cuirass that flattens
my breasts, just as wise old Longinus does,

while the peacocks fan their ass-eyes at us
and shriek. The Romans will let me live, he says,
as all things have been let for me to do,
as I was let to leave the hut where my father hid
the girl children he'd keep

and trade the softness of sheep for rough
satin sheets. And my people? People know
nothing but the flicker of the fire mouth
and the dictates of the stars while our
aristocrats who stood me up

against the riches of Rome, beg another stand.

They know those devil djinns are

the dust of an hundred columns, and that fortune

is the only god; that gold is measured out

in bones. We have come a long way

since the "best men" of Miletus lit their city

with living torches of the poor:

we have learned to oppress ourselves,

and squeeze out lucre to grease the gears

that trip the mouth

that swallows us whole.

ODYSSEUS' SCAR

Wouldn't we all like to be recognized

by our old nurse

as the hero

from a childhood scar

I think

in the bathroom at work

in front of the big mirror

on election day.

As Auerbach's *Mimesis* explains

the story is flattened

into the image

from the washing of the feet

to the accident of the hunt,

on a visit to his grandfather,

Autolycus,

the wolf, himself.

My own boar-tusk gash is only

a pockmark, just above

my left eyebrow, my hunt

the oatmeal bath

and the room with the wicker

fold-out and the wallpaper

of red scallops

and the white monkey

holding a ball; in a black cardigan
and blue pants, I am my own
nurse, and I barely know
myself.

It's election day,
how did it go?

PARTY CITY

Apropos of nothing I am thinking
about "the death fall," forty-feet
onto a hard surface like concrete.
The abruptness and the speed,
Walter Matthau dropping
like a sack at the end of *Charade,*
maybe time enough to think,
"I'm so fucked," and scream.
There are other falls, endless ones,
where every foot is death,
but the bottom is always receding.

On my phone screen
A.G. Barr's pixelated head
settles like a jowly mountain
of green-gray putty on his shoulders
thick-framed glasses
an ill-made disguise
or like those frames added
to humanize the empty, eyeless void
of a Muppet. Rosenstein, behind
and away, is the very orange of a Muppet,
and all eye, lid upon lid upon lid.

I watch their mouths moving

on mute, a kind of terror-flapping,

a black hole, a silent

scream. Yes, this is the death fall,

with no end. Something

brushes up against me,

it is a woman in the morning crush,

smart suit, business casual. What strikes

me are two overstuffed bags

held tight in her hand,

they are unduly light for their size,

nearly floating, the bags read

PARTY CITY,

they are bright foil balloons,

and if she loosened her grip

even a little, they would

dip out of their bags

fall upward, like a soul, zooming past

Grand Central's oversized

American flag, up to the vaulted dome,

new stars in those famed constellations

a cheeky wag, a life-fall

against all that is bad.

MEMENTO

They have blown the bridge

behind the bridge

into the water. The girders

that described its span

rest upon the lips

of barges, still formed.

Concrete pylons vaporized.

Gone. I can't understand

why they leave it, broken,

kneeling on the river,

a steel net, an old scar.

You ask me if it's your fault.

It sounds so much better in French,

don't you think? *Est ce de ma faute?*

Of course it is, all of it:

The sun on the snow, the beaver dam,

the red osiers. It is exactly the same,

physiologists say,

to remember the past

as it is to imagine a future.

Except for this body that we suppose

our history has written upon

such words

of guilt . . . No one will tell you,

"I absolve you."

There are no gods to say

you must take an oar

upon your back and walk inland

until no one

can recognize it.

Set it, anyway,

in a cairn. The strangers

of that place will call it

a "winnowing fan."

The wheat of your life

will slide along the blade,

and the chaff—

the chaff will blow away.

From the Earth, for its Creatures

Animula, vagula, blandula
Hospes comesque corporis
Quae nunc abibis in loca
Pallidula, rigida, nudula
Nec, ut soles, dabis iocos.

—

Little vagabond, charming soul,
My body's companion, partner,
Whither thou now? To a place
Colorless, hard, and bare.
No more of your joking, there.

—Emperor Hadrian,
138 CE

NOTES

A NOTE ON THE TYPE: The body text of this book is set in ADOBE CASLON, a revival designed by Carol Twombly after studying the output of William Caslon's foundry from 1734 (when his Latin typeface was "fully realized") through 1770. Caslon's first designed typefaces were "exotics," an Arabic in 14pt, made on behalf of the Society for Promoting Christian Knowledge; a Hebrew; and a Coptic.

The headers and the section titles are set in TRAJAN, another typeface designed by Twombly; a "crisp" and "faithful" translation of the letterforms of the Roman inscription at the base of Trajan's column in Rome.

S O U R C E S : Adobe and Wikipedia.

This entire collection might be better entitled "Memoirs of the Trump Administration."

ANIMAL

"EASTER Scene," is real, although my carving of the lamb is a memory of my uncle or father in the small, dark dining room of grandmother's farmhouse, with the bone-handled carver, and the general atmosphere of gin-and-tonics and *Virginia Slims.*

"The Light" has come in many different shapes. The grafting of the creation legend onto the simple observation of the way the morning arrives in many layers is, and the connection of it to that moment after a sudden rainstorm when the clouds open up, is, perhaps, awkward. But I love the fire saved in a reed, and the muskrat reaching deep as it can for us. We animals are in this all together, to our benefit and others' detriment.

We lived in an old house on the shoulder of a hill, on a fairly low-trafficked road; it was a blacksmith's quarters from an old 18th c. farm that had had a new addition in the 90s. In the oldest parts of the house were strange chills, and cluster flies beating against single-pane glass. We used to walk up and down the hill, and once found "A Fox," it must have been hit overnight. We were going through a very stressful period in our lives.

There is a "Rodeo Monkey," he's called "Whiplash the Cowboy Monkey." He was born in 1987, in Florida, and rides a border collie. I saw a picture once of a furry monkey riding an enormous bull in an arena somewhere in India. I think it became something of a meme. Of course he would have an ego large enough to refer to himself in the third person.

"The Octopus" is a marvel. Their suckers instantly release upon feeling their own flesh so as to keep their many, independently acting limbs from knotting up. A video shows an octopus, on a ship, over what seems like an excruciatingly long time slither, flattened, across the deck, and squeezing itself through a tiny hole in the hull and out into the ocean.

We had a math teacher in high school one of my friends said reminded him of Tiny Tim; the friend used to sing "Tiptoe Through the Tulips" at me before class started. The teacher, it turned out, was passing notes to the girls in the class, complimenting them on their dress and appearance. The girls were 12 and 13. I only found this out much later. I do not remember Tiny Tim from "The Great American Circus," just one languid python, but Dad does.

I passed "King Rat" once on a rain-soaked day, in Bed Stuy. It was a regal creature, it had a regal death. The next time I walked by, it was gone, leaving just a red crown stained into the concrete.

I find the sight of "Blood" makes me unbearably queasy; it's even worse to see my own. Not doctor material here, no. What's more disconcerting is how watery it is, it trembles in the vial like the ocean. I think my generation may have been the last to have a projector wheeled in to the classroom to watch old educational films, and cartoons.

I want the recent spate of "Thylacine" sightings to be real so badly. It is not so much as it may have been once for me, the mystery of it, but more the injustice of man-made extinction. What right have we to strip the world of its beauties, one by one. There is no escape from it, though. "Nothing gold can stay." Art, poetry, love, all a shabby substitute for the infinite complexity of a muscle tensed under bristling fur.

"The Invisible Bridge" is just that, like the silly, clear bridge that carried Indiana Jones to the chamber with the grail cup. It is a real photo of a bear jumping, hind feet first, into the water, you might Google it. It is also a book by Rick Perlstein about the rise of Reagan, embodiment of what Khrushchev told Nixon: if the people believe in an imaginary river, "you don't tell them there's no river there. You build an imaginary bridge over the imaginary river."

In "William Harvey's Dogs" the country doctor is the one who rambled through Dylan's "Love Minus Zero/No Limit." It was entitled "Vivisection," first. People are usually killed by their own guns, I have read.

"Bee-Father" — The emperor Diocletian, who reformed the administration of the Roman empire and stabilized it after a tumultuous century also was unique in abdicating the throne. In his decade of retirement, he delighted in gardening, and was especially proud of his cabbages. Bees have been lauded for the organization of their society. There are many folkloric traditions around bees, and a long history of their association with the muses, and with poetry. I grew up on what was once part of a large farm in a hollow called Winnie Hollow, between Honey Hill and East Hill, where Allen Ginsburg's *Committee on Poetry* owned a farmhouse and 80 acres.

"Moth Money" — I have a money-clip style wallet, and bills wind up crumpled through taking it in and out of my pocket. Our cat Sadie likes to carry them through the house in her mouth. I see the bills pop out like the moths in empty wallets from old cartoons, those from the 30s; dark and bright, and ugly with stereotypes.

There is nothing so wild that a suburban professional can't be flown out to kill it, and stuff it, and mount it. I cannot get the image of a small live fish pierced through with an outsized hook, twirling in open air on the end of a line, "People Watching" as it dies.

"The Lotto" as it is played across America, in expensive scratch-offs and delusive jackpots, is in some respects one of the more cruel human institutions, in our enlightened age, taking from the have-nots and padding the budgets of the haves, trading on hope. The spark of sunlight through plastic is as hard as the bloom of an uncalled-for memory. Life can be difficult, when just by living we are complicit in so much suffering. The odds of winning a jackpot are not statistically improved by purchasing a ticket.

"This is Fine, Dog" is what I call the genial, and thoroughly-in-denial character from a 2013 K.C. Green cartoon that has become a flourishing meme. He has googly eyes, a toothy grin, and a jaunty little hat. His house is on fire, and he continues to assert that "things are going to be okay" as the flesh falls off his bones. Same, Dog, same.

VEGETABLE

I T'S best to eschew "Tree Repair." Sealing off wounds just seals in rot. Their woody bodies continue to challenge our understanding, for example, there is no good physical explanation, so I've read, of how water is drawn up from the roots to the top. Studies have shown trees must have a rudimentary store of memory, somewhere, which they use, at a minimum, to count days and remember past seasons. Trees live best in large, interconnected societies, which we thin and disrupt.

"SUN Worship" was the text I saw on a church sign in Brooklyn. I like the sun/son echo, which is, somehow, a very Frazerian take on Christianity. My favorite moment is the birds at the taco. The word "clever" makes its way over from the *Jurassic Park* movie, when one character says of one of the birds' carnivorous ancestors, "clever girl!" The Roman general Varus was ambushed in the Teutoburg Forest by an alliance of German tribes. His legions were cut to pieces and their eagle standards taken.

I was reading Dumezil's *Gods of the Ancient Northmen* on "The Death of Balder" and also rereading Frazer of *The Golden Bough*, while being devoured by mosquitos in the yard below our apartment in Bed Stuy now more than a few summers ago. I bought a little grill and two chairs at Family Dollar. The times were more innocent, but still suffused with dread.

At "Almost 9pm" one night I observed that our hanging plant, when you water it, a bit later the tips of the leaves extrude these perfect spherical droplets. They are like crystal, and sometimes I'll stare into them. You won't see the future, just a twisted view of the room and your own flesh reflected.

These are the names of actual ancient "Shipwrecks" from an essay by Patrice Pomey, "Les conséquences de l'évolution des techniques de construction navale sur l'économie maritime antique: quelques exemples," on archaeological discoveries as they relate to ancient maritime technologies. Since French doesn't come easily to me, I found myself falling into a sort of hypnosis as I worked through the paragraphs on the subway.

Since the first time I cut "Last Cut" I have recut it probably a dozen times. It was the title poem of my first chapbook which was printed by Hamilton College. The poem has grown and shrunk over the years, but I've never quite shaken it. Its ideal form would, I think, be a haiku. Something like:

> *A quiet fall day.*
> *Lawnmower clips the apple.*
> *Red springs into snow.*

"Security Questions" was a poem co-authored by NBT Bank, N.A.

"Catastrophe" — Well it all is, isn't it, just one big, slow motion catastrophe. A line from another poem "some make of it more, others less." The poem came about because of my cousin Jonathan's Greek wife, Evi, who couldn't stop laughing, imitating the American pronunciation, with its exaggerated, and wrongly stressed, central flat-"a" sound, of the Greek word for an "overturning, a sudden end."

We bought a house in 2017. It's "Home," and for many years of renting and travel the concept has been far less physical to me than it is now, again.

"Milkweed" was a poem called "Maude," before, but I think I have the focus right now. Toni taught me about gems, their cuts, and settings, and together we first noticed the beauty of the milkweed flower on the hill of our property in Roseboom.

"A Short History of Financial Euphoria" is the title of a small volume by the economist John Kenneth Galbraith which has short chapters on historical bubbles and collapses, including the South Sea Bubble, the ramp up to the Great Depression, and Tulipomania, in the Netherlands. The poem once referenced "sensible" economists, the Friedmanites who saw their star rise in the 70s and 80s but horribly missed the most recent housing bubble and its consequences. Galbraith, much maligned as overly qualitative, and perhaps tainted by his involvement in the New Deal and the success of his "popular" works like *The Affluent Society,* seems more than any of his peers to have gotten something right about the nature of our economy.

"Say It to the Mountain" might have something of the spiritual, I am convinced we sang once in music class, and of course something of "if the mountain will not come to Muhammad" a phrase I picture most vividly coming from Orson Welles as Rochester in *Jane Eyre.* The scene of the poem mostly happened. I despise people who cavalierly disregard animal suffering, and despise myself for not doing more. There is the vegetable feeling, of helplessness. In the end, Jesus, behaving pretty much, as Betrand Russell points out, like a real jerk, withered the fig tree for not doing what it could not do: produce fruit out of season.

The moment "The Bride Extrudes," in her dress, comes, I realize, from Cocetau's *La Belle et la Bête.*…What is it about high places on a clear, cool day when the wind whips past? You feel yourself growing up, leaving your body behind. Transforming into something different. If only for a moment.

If "The Trees on the Island (in the River)" think of us, they think poorly of us, unrooted, tossed here and there across the earth, like refuse. Unfree. This poem makes me think of Maurice Sendak, for some reason I can't put my finger on. Let the wild rumpus begin!

I can't seem to give up on "Meditations," the first poem I wrote after nearly a decade of not writing at all, as unsuccessful as it continues to be. I wanted to use the word "serried" for the Greek letters Marcus Aurelius scratched on the parchment but couldn't make it fit. At the end, he is contravening the advice of the "mysteries," and drinking from the waters of Lethe. Despite what the text of his *Meditations* says, I read in it a tired soul who wants to forget. The footnotes, as elsewhere, as always, are more aesthetic than informational.

I love the dagger (†) best. [I did end up making "serried" work, so change continues, unabated.]

"Hollow" — I grew up on Winnie Hollow Road. Of course, there is a ghost. The beaver dam in the lower field is impressive. Such diligent engineers, creating a spillway for pressure relief, beavers, in damming a stream, refashion a landscape more than any other animal, save man.

MINERAL

"GRAND Opening" is not based on an actual event, though something like it may have happened, it's more of a feeling. The little clocks ticking along are Leibnitz's *monads*. In his philosophy, the world of souls exists alongside the world of bodies, both moving along, obeying natural laws. It is only by the coincidence of action that we appear to have control.

"Mycenae"'s ten years ago, is more than a decade and a half now [now twenty?]. Back before the Euro, ECB, IMF. The fires weren't in the streets of Athens, but in the olive groves. The fires have died down, but the misery remains. *Et in Arcadia ego.*

"Six of One..." — Scene: The *Whole Foods* in Columbus Circle; you descend the escalator as though on a voyage to Hell.

"Biography" started from a comment someone made that a person's story is always the same: the hero is born at the beginning and dies at the end. The biographies are made up, but the problems are real.

"I Have" far fewer notes this time around, on these poems. I wonder if it's because many of them are new, and I've had less time to live with the ideas in them, or maybe they are lesser poems, with fewer ideas, or maybe they're better poems, communicating the ineffable. I know I've stripped references from them I would have left in, before. Do I like them, do I hate them? Both.

Someone commented that poems about coffee are "common"…and "Grounds" is one. At any rate, the advice is sound: for a French press grind to the consistency of breadcrumbs, and wait 30 seconds before pouring the water, stir when it's half full.

I was "Reading *Lear*" for the first time, right before Trump's election, on a long flight from Hong Kong to JFK. *By the pricking of my thumbs...*

"Two Years Before the Mast" is a terrific book about a long sea journey, about the restorative power of sheer physical labor, about life at sea. I felt very connected to it during the time I talk about.

"The White Supremacist (and I)" is, apparently, our new life (and our old life though many, and I, fooled ourselves into a complacent self-satisfaction: "America is already great," or was it).

"Yahoo! Answers" was a real thing, it almost seemed new, once. Now it's as old as the pyramids, a monumental shambles. I've done a few poems in this vein, is it flarf? Maybe.

"Roger Ailes is Dead." Enough said.

I first encountered the story of the "Seven Sleepers" in Gibbon. The abridged editions of *The Decline and Fall* generally go lighter on the last three volumes, which cover the Eastern Empire, and the rise of Islam. I recommend them, though, and every imperfect, idiosyncratic, monumental line and footnote of it. The sleepers were seven youths of Ephesus accused of Christianity during the Decian persecution. Instead of recanting, they renounced their possessions, and fell into a long slumber, only to awake to Christianity's triumph. The Qur'an adds a faithful dog to the story.

בתזבי : *Btzby*, pronounced Bat-Zabbai, called "Zenobia," after the death of her husband, the King of Palmyra, ca. 267 CE, taking personal and vigorous leadership, expanded the Palmyran empire from Syria to Egypt and Anatolia, controlling the most important trade routes from the East to Rome. Only a few years later, she either perished after being led in golden chains through Rome in the Emperor Aurelian's triumph, or lived out her days as a rich matron on the Appian way. She is supposed to have claimed descent from Cleopatra and Dido.

"Odysseus' Scar" was recognized by his aged nurse, who knew him for the hero despite his goddess-bestowed disguise as a beggar. We all have our own signature scar, whether it's on the inside or the out. The porcelain monkey with the ball belonged to my grandmother; Elvis owned the same one, it has pride of place at Graceland. Where we have hope that we all will be received.

"Party City" might be the saddest two-word phrase. It ought to be a thrilling thing, fun, but it's just an empty bag, a big box store, stuffed with joy that has been suffocated in cellophane. Still, who doesn't love a bright, metallic balloon, filled with helium, gently tugging to be free?

The collection ends with a little "Memento." It is also an Odysseus-inspired poem. He was called on to expiate his sins by making an offering of an oar deep in a landlocked country. A winnowing fan is used to separate the edible wheat from the hard chaff after it has been beaten with a flail on the threshing floor. There is an oblique reference to the 2000 film of the same name. The French from when I was making a half-hearted effort to bone up on the language during my commute, the bridge of course is the old Tappan Zee.

♦ ♦♦♦ ♦♦♦ ♦ ♦♦♦ ♦♦♦ ♦

I hope you have enjoyed this small, poetic journey through the known universe:

✳ A N I M A L ❦ V E G E T A B L E ✧ M I N E R A L

ACKNOWLEDGMENTS

Poems in this collection first appeared, in one form or another, in the following publications:

ANIMAL

"Easter Scene" appears in *Chicago Quarterly Review,* Vol. 26, February 2018.

"The Light" appeared in *The Evansville Review,* 2020.

"Rodeo Monkey" was published in *Pamplemousse,* Vol. 3, No. 2, Spring 2016.

"The Octopus" appeared in *Lime Hawk,* Issue 9, June 2016.

"The Great American Circus" was published online at *Queen Mob's Tea House,* July 12, 2016.

"King Rat" was featured on *The Madison Review: the Extended Cut* No. 3, October 29, 2018.

"Thylacine" was in *Matter* Issue 22, February 2018.

"The Invisible Bridge" appeared on *Entropy,* December 20, 2019.

"William Harvey's Dogs" was published in *Dead King Magazine,* Issue 3, July 2016.

"Moth Money" was published in *Jelly Bucket* #7, Spring 2017.

"This is Fine, Dog" appeared on *Entropy,* December 20, 2019.

VEGETABLE

"Tree Repair" was published in *The Birds We Piled Loosely,* Issue 9, October 2016.

"SUN Worship" is in *The Harpoon Review,* Issue 31, from April 2017.

"The Death of Balder" is part of Whistling Shade Press's 2016 *Shades of Myth* chapbook.

"Almost 9pm" appears in the collection *KILL YR DARLINGS; TWEET YR DRAFTS (mediocre love poems),* June 2016.

"Shipwrecks" is in *Common Ground Review* Fall/Winter 2017.

"Last Cut" is the title poem of my chapbook *Last Cut* (2000,

Trustees of Hamilton College).

"Security Questions" can be found in *Adirondack Review*, Spring 2017.

"Catastrophe" was featured on *Two Cities Review*, Issue 20, Winter 2018. (And nominated for a *Pushcart Prize.*)

"Home" appeared on *Streetlight* online, August 25, 2017.

"Milkweed" (then-titled "Maude") was published in *The Round*, Issue XIV, May 2016.

"A Short History of Financial Euphoria" was first printed in *Pamplemousse*, Vol. 3, No. 2, Spring 2016.

"The Bride Extrudes" was published in *Big Muddy, A Journal of the Mississippi River Valley*, Volume 16.2, Spring 2017.

"Say it to the Mountain" is in *Magnolia Review, Vol. 6, Issue 1*, January 2020.

"Hollow" appeared in *Alabama Literary Review*, Volume 26, 2017.

MINERAL

"Grand Opening" is in *Saranac Review* No. 15, 2019-2020.

"Biography" was featured in the 2018 *Sanskrit Literary-Arts Magazine.*

"Grounds" was published in *Straight Forward Poetry* Issue 16, February 2018.

"I Have" appeared in *Streetlight* online, August 25, 2017.

"The White Supremacist (and I)" was published in *The Round*, Spring 2018.

"Yahoo! Answers" appeared in *Tahoma Literary Review*, Issue 6, March 2016.

"Seven Sleepers" was published in *Straight Forward Poetry* Issue 16, February 2018.

"Odysseus' Scar" is online at *Juked*, tagged [distinguisher], June 30, 2019.

"Party City" is in *Magnolia Review, Vol. 6, Issue 1*, January 2020.

"Memento" is featured in *Poet Lore*, Volume 114 Number 3/4, Fall/Winter 2019.

ACKNOWLEDGMENTS
(CONT'D)

T HANKS, first and foremost, to Toni Hacker, my dearest, my love, whose creative talents far outstrip mine, and with whom I am lucky to share a beautiful home and a beautiful life. You support me and enrich me in every respect. You are a creator of the first order, and an inspiration. <3 And to my parents Bruce and Barbara who brought me up with love, and a love of nature.

Thanks also, to Twitter, that glittering cesspool, that bright pit, nattering, chattering land which has tested my soul, but unlocked a creative spark that had been languishing. And to all my friends, there, real and imagined.

To @dril, who showed before anyone that real poetry was possible in this age.

But I owe the greatest thanks to those who have read, enjoyed, and encouraged my poetry. In particular, Mark Mastroianni, whose kind words and incomparably beautiful gift of art inspired me to assemble this collection.

Also to my brother Sam Harnett, who writes with sound, and to John Durkin, chef, mayor, and songwriter; to Frank Stock, who was the first to carry me to the beauties of language, and whom I always hope to make proud. To George O'Connell, my college writing professor, and a terrific poet and translator. To Sandra Simonds, who read and commented on many of these poems in an earlier form. Thanks also to @dntsqzthchrmn for #TwitterPoetryClub.

To Tom Blodgett carpenter, to Lynn Talbot painter; to Karl Steel. To Colin Dickey. To L. Nichols and Christina Chestnut. To Joseph Howley. To (Aunt) Diane Margaritis, and to Rebecca Woodson. To the other supporters of my work, and this volume in particular: Jonathan Rury, Howard Mittelmark (I hope the novel I sent you isn't too unbearable), Guan Yang, Stephanie Theodore, Alden Golab, Mikhail Shnaydman; to Eileen Ridge, Mary Brennan, Sue Jones, Anne Trubek in the Rust Belt, to Elizabeth Peik and Bashir Abdallah (Cherry Valley forever), to Ashley Strosnider in farthest Nebraska, to Sarah Miers, Robyn Hayes; to Jonathan Schwarzberg and Lance Yeager.

To the misdemeanor outlaw, chased an' cheated by pursuit; to the gentle, to the kind, to the guardians and protectors of the mind. The unpawned painter beyond his rightful time. To the aching ones whose wounds cannot be nursed. To every hung-up person in the whole wide universe.